Prayer for the Little City

Books by Sydney Lea

POETRY

No Sign
(1987)

The Floating Candles
(1982)

Searching the Drowned Man
(1980)

FICTION

A Place in Mind
(1989)

CRITICISM

The Burdens of Formality:
Essays on the Poetry of Anthony Hecht (editor)
(1989)

PRAYER FOR THE LITTLE CITY

—

Poems by

—

SYDNEY LEA

CHARLES SCRIBNER'S SONS
New York

Charles Scribner's Sons
Macmillan Publishing Company
866 Third Avenue, New York, NY 10022
Collier Macmillan Canada, Inc.

Library of Congress Cataloging-in-Publication Data
Lea, Sydney, 1942–
    Prayer for the little city: poems / by Sydney Lea.
      p. cm.
    ISBN 0-684-19129-6
    I. Title.
PS3562.E16P73   1990   89-38387   CIP
811'.54—dc20

The author would like to thank the editors of the following periodicals for permission to reprint several of these poems, which (sometimes in slightly different versions) originally appeared in their pages: *The Kenyon Review,* "Six Sundays Toward a Seventh"; *The Laurel Review,* "Two Chets"; *Prairie Schooner,* "Pietà" and "Late Season"; *The Gettysburg Review,* "Roadside, February"; *Grand Street,* "Pianissimo"; *Crazyhorse,* "On Munson Island"; *The Missouri Review,* "Sun, Rising"; *Poetry,* "Over Brogno"; *The New Yorker,* "Another Autumn, And"; *Antaeus,* "For Faith"; *The Partisan Review,* "Manifest"; *The Georgia Review,* "Museum," *Verse,* "D-Day Ode for Dean," "Amputee."
Thanks also to the John Simon Guggenheim Memorial Foundation.

10   9   8   7   6   5   4   3   2   1

Printed in the United States of America

For Amico John Barone, and for my mother

Fanno sempre bella figura.

Contents

Prayer for the Little City

I. SIX SUNDAYS TOWARD A SEVENTH

1. *Do not trust in these deceptive words:* 3
2. *February—winter! lightning! thunder!* 5
3. *In cold what we see are the parson's wraithy breaths* 7
4. *Locked though we were in our own sick, aching flesh* 9
5. *Guy and Robert do it the older way:* 11
6. *The shroud of white is leaching from* 13
7. *Still dark when we file like children out on the turf,* 15

II. MANIFEST

Two Chets 19
At the Flyfisher's Shack 22
Clouded Evening, Late September 24
Questions of Empathy Way Upstate 26
Pietà 28
For the Solitary 31
Late Season 33
Roadside, February 35
Manifest 38

III. MUSEUM

Pianissimo 43
On Munson Island 45
Museum 48
D-Day Ode for Dean 51
Winter Tournament 53
Amputee 55

vii

CONTENTS

Sun, Rising 58

Over Brogno 60

Another Autumn, And 65

For Faith 68

PRAYER FOR THE LITTLE CITY

—January 6

Hushed plane, the pond. Ice-fishers' lights. Still little city.
Men hug their whiskey jugs inside as they loiter among
whiffs of bait, potbelly smoke, sock-wool and sweat.

Laconic chat: an idle joke; or God damn that
or God damn this, although such words aren't even angry,
but ordinary. Snowmobile roads thread our shacks

one to another; now and then, Big Lou throws open
his door (like an oven's, infernal within) and cries to a neighbor,
"Doin' some good?" Or dirty Duane, the one we call

"Blackfly," will call words much the same and the neighborhood
will rally from silence a moment or two, then sink back in.
It's half past ten. Blackfly and Lou and all the quietened

others stay through the darkness till dawn, whether or not
the small smelt bite. What *of* this town, this bob-house crew?
What of Ben, who's outside skimming his ice-hole's **o**'s?

He sniffs and blows, thinks vaguely of women, and thinks to name
some part of their bodies out loud across the frozen surface:
a shout all worthless, directionless, a shout all shoddy

with platitude, devoid of embrace, containing nothing,
not even longing . . . at least for sex. Just part of a mood
and situation much at odds, it might be imagined,

with a hopeful season, season of gods, of resolution
to start anew. Outside, the flags on their planted poles
in the utter chill are utterly slack, betraying no

visionary   prey down under   to clasp our lures.
The dullness is pure.   No signs, no wonders,   no mystery . . .
except it be   the care with which   all night men linger,

as if in prayer   for a novel fish,   or a novel way
by which to address   some thing they're feeling.   Surely this is
part of what holds us   under crude ceilings   beaded with pitch,

amid this fetor   with speechless friends.   Surely, surely
a sense that early,   before the dawn   (or sooner, or later)
our flags will all   at once, together,   tremble and shimmy.

Epiphany   —o bright palaver!   o every hole
a yodel of steam!   So runs our fancy   in the absence of sound
in this merest of towns,   although our shanties'   very beams

of light seem bored.   O little city,   we think, it's cold;
city, how still,   how still we see thee.   Still, the stars
go by above,   even here,   and still may love

embrace the year.

I

Six Sundays
Toward a Seventh

(21 FEBRUARY–3 APRIL, 1988)

—for the Reverend Malcolm Grobe

*If during meditation our thoughts move to persons
who are near to us or to those we are concerned about,
then let them linger there.*

—DIETRICH BONHOEFFER, *Meditating On the Word*

I

Do not trust in these
deceptive words:

This is the temple of the Lord,
The temple of the Lord. . . .
First Lenten Sunday, and the Jeremiad

Reduces us to heretics,
Quite properly: the temple draws us inward
Yet again. "Quebec Express"

—The wind along our glacial reach of river—
Penetrates through nailholes, sockets.
The fellowship, however, gathers.

Till service starts, we throw clichés at winter,
Chatting to unlock it,
Warm ourselves. The litany assures,

Its scope so narrow:
Oh yes, we say and pray, they'll all be here:
Jonquils; jobs; the chanting thrush; the sparrow . . . .

Blooms and babies, issues of the town.
How spring will nap the lawns.
Someone's good news to celebrate—

Remission. Calm. Some novel revenue
To keep the school afloat:
"Revenue," says Blaise: "The coming back."

It's not such puns nor platitudes that soothe
But how they do come back.
Not peace, we're warned. *A sword.*

Not, thus, to trust in children, flowers, birds?
Nor mist all raiment-soft on open water?
And not these words, nor pungency of lumber

That fell, before last fall, before the blade?
It isn't them we trust in any case
But their return, as sure as ours.

The season's myth declines to death,
And yet again, again, we park our cars
And move inside to speak our faith.

—JEREMIAH 7:4;
—MATTHEW 10:34

2

February—winter! lightning! thunder!

Blotched with passion, his girlish fingers
Clenched the wood on the back of the bench before him:
Flood made us late. We straggled in and saw him.

Stranger than Sunday's storm, this praying stranger
Who, when at last he straightened, turned to observe us,
It grew more rude than odd, his manner:

Jane, who bakes for Communion Service,
He reckoned over-dressed. He looked askance.
But he wrinkled his nose as well at the threadbare suit

Of Harley, everyone's friend, and his callused hands.
He scowled at Vernon the deacon, storekeeper, farmer,
Huge in gumboots—feisty, hirsute,

With a voice to front this freakish thunder.
Lightning galloped, insistent; untimely, rain
Smote the clerestory's stained memorial panes

For Ed—our late and moderate moderator.
God love us, a person might think, if this were The Christ,
Returned as it says He means to return.

The hymn begun, the voice of the guest
Had doubtless heft. (It soared in fact over Vernon's.)
Ended, polite, we asked him to make himself known.

He named no name. He said, instead: "I present you
The text of the morning: *Even the dust of your town*
That clings to our feet we wipe off against you. . . ."

And *"I saw Satan fall like lightning*
From heaven." The wanderer rose with that, departed.
    "And we let the bastard preach, by God Almighty!"

So Vernon swears, as we talk on Monday about it,
Though surely he knows that ours is a common anger.
In fury, he flings his goods on the shelves:

He can't think surely that *I* will differ
In wrath at such an intruder—troublemaker!—
On us who love our neighbors, as much as ourselves.

—LUKE: 10–11;
— ————: 10:17;
— ————: 10:28

6

3

In cold what we see are the
parson's wraithy breaths:

There are some standing here who will not taste death
Before they see His kingdom come with power.
> *. . . Jesus took with him Peter*

And James and John and led them up a mountain
—Where is the heat?—*and he was transfigured before them.*
> I think of John my brother,

Distorting Scripture. We all should huddle together.
The frozen organ flats as a spirit might do.
> I mumble: "I took with me two . . . ,"

Blaspheming. One was John, and Blaise the other.
We three crossed a mountain and down to a river.
> In that photograph of Montana:

Around my John, transforming him, an aura.
The light is low, it's near the fall, it's evening.
> Upstream he stands, feasting

On trout from an iron skillet, head and all.
That inchoate pattern on the scarp's bronze wall—
> A handful of geese inscribing

Its *mene, mene, tekel* and *parsin*. Departing.
So many, the things of this world. I took up the camera.
> The river boiled and stammered.

We heard coyotes at gossip, and bugling elk.
And there was something else that Blaise and I felt
    More than we saw, as John,

With his fish and some wine, profane in the dying sun,
Feasted and drank and gloried in *gold and silver,*
    Standing there upriver.

World: *bronze, iron, wood, stone.*
Blaise, and I, and all of these, and John,
    And the heat of the breath that was coming,

As we shivered together there, and a greater something.
A bear coughed, sudden and near, unseen overhead.
And we shivered, standing there, with awe, undead.

                    —MARK, 9:1, 2;
                    —DANIEL, 5:23–26

4

Locked though we were in our
own sick, aching flesh,

All night we tended our newborn as she squalled.
My eyes open hot. The whited chains of drool
Fasten her milk-blistered pout to my wife's left breast.

I must depart them, the slumbering woman and daughter,
Bound—or is it released?—in consciouslessness.
I make my hobbled, pedestrian rounds to the others:

Each child, however the mean dark's trials were protracted,
Is set in peace in the body now, it appears.
I could if I would fix all in a picture, and call it

Free and Serene. I teeter in front of a chair,
Inclined as I am at once to surrender and fight,
Blessing and cursing lame joints and labored breath.

In a cupboard, caffeine—a drug precisely right
Or wrong. My thick-boned hand is a quake on the shelf.
Inside, outside, upward, downward, death.

A redpoll, one of the daily many misguided,
Has struck a pane. The twitch of its remnant talons:
Sad as spastic's dancing. There beside it,

A blood-mustachio'd cat now contemplates,
Lion-lazy and -lordly, tenantless space.
What can it see in such air, as dim as dungeons'?

False spring's ice has flayed our Flowering Crab.
Daniel asserts: *He rescues and delivers.*
So, at the service this morning, it will be read;

Well, let them read, how his God *works signs and wonders,*
On heaven and earth. At home I rest unassured,
And side with that side of Paul the Letter-Writer,

Late out of prison, which claims he *would depart,*
Claims he *would be with Christ, for that is far better. . . .*
Shut in self-pity, I'd disregard how he added,

To be in the flesh is more needful on your account;
Or how Jesus chided a lame one, *Take up your pallet,*
Breaking the Sabbath, commending our worldly rounds.

—DANIEL, 6:27;

—PHILIPPIANS, 1:23, 24

5
Guy and Robert do it the older way:

Single pails, draft horse and sleigh.
No garish plastic tubing. No four-wheel drive.
Fifth Lenten Sabbath—a sugaring day.

By your endurance you will gain your lives.
Last night's chill moon, blue stars and blasts of aurora
Seemed wonders in darkness, powers.

But we're not yet there. The morning's fair.
Robert and Guy, with Joli, their great blond gelding,
Slave in the damp corned snow.

Or say they endure.
"Slave"—that shouldn't be the word,
Since lo, these generations ago,

Uprose the maple trade against manumission:
Brute harvests of cane
By blacks on steaming southern plantations.

How might so white a March be further from that?
(Oh yes, there's the steam,
In plumes above the infernal sugar shack,

And shimmering over the frames of the men and Joli.)
No one should live like a beast. . . .
A new dawn's breaking, and we're enjoined to be ready,

Lest that day come upon you suddenly.
I think of the trees,
Of acid winging in on rain from the west,

Coming in a cloud. Can it be a sign?
The maples persist in sweetness,
And Guy and Robert in archaic business,

And there will be signs in stars and sun and moon.
St. Paul ponders the doom of those
With minds set on earthly things,

And our pastor recites the warnings of Luke 21.
What is the part of these laborers in snow?
The Day may be coming soon, but until then . . .

—LUKE 21

—PHILIPPIANS 3:19

6

The shroud of white is leaching from

The village common. The ragged humble return
To aim their Geiger counters over mud.
What has frost thrown up?

Keys to no door, bent coins, drained cans
And foil—aluminum:
Bright as angels, devoid of value,

History-less. Still Jim and Mickey wave.
Their women smoke in a relic GMC. . . .
At church now Harley reads

The proper Scripture, smoothing out the page:
You'll always have them with you,
The poor, deluded Mickeys, Jims,

The whey-faced wives . . . who might be better off,
I've thought, if they could sit among us here.
Alone in awkward prayer

—In which I name whatever haunts me Love—
Can I invite them in:
The spirit is willing, but the flesh is weak.

The Palms of welcome lie on the spotless altar,
Limp. *Ride On, Ride On, In Majesty;*
Let this cup pass from me—

In mind, the song and Gospel swim together
As silly clicks and beeps
Outside suggest some other find,

13

Unblessed. Three times I've passed these common seekers:
Once, as I rode down to buy the *Times,*
Again on my way home,

And last arriving here, a week from Easter—
Passed them as if blind
In study of corrupted masks of snow.

I will strike the shepherd, the sheep will be scattered.
So was it prophesied.
And as he spoke the cock began to crow.

—MATTHEW 26

7

Still dark when we file like
children out on the turf,

Yet our hymn is *For the Beauty of the Earth.*
Irony scourges. Is that how grown-ups atone?
The apostate, Jack, is back with us. It's cancer.

We've gathered, we few others, by the river
For other reasons, whatever. Where's the sun?
Sunrise Service. Easter. Ice on the waters.

In the flow, among black limbs, a jug bobs past us,
Empty, thrown perhaps by a drunken angler
Who waited through last fall but never caught him,

The fish he'd prayed for, childlike—unseeable, awesome.
We here know life is hard but for some promise.
We murmur *For the Love which from our birth. . . .*

Debris, relentless, eddies down from north.
I imagine the fisherman, grown more doubtful than Thomas:
One dusk he flung away the jug, the dream.

Is that a Christmas present, still in its carton?
Over and around us lies, we sing.
We have mouthed the store-bought dough, the bitter wine.

They are real enough, the wounds we've seen.
Last Wednesday, shocked, we buried redoubtable Vernon.
We'd all feel different, maybe, in different weather.

It would seem somehow less *willed,* this banding together.
We have left undone the things we ought to have done,
And the other way round. Jane's at the clinic. Neurosis.

Harley's halt again. Accursed phlebitis.
Flotsam—fragmented story—drifts and spins.
What was it that the Samaritan woman said?

A man who told me all I ever did.
The pastor opened by reading about her from John.
Lazarus too. And the blind man's pool at Silóam.

As a fish-eye sun slides open over the mountain,
Our children strain to break from us and play.
We end with *This our hymn of grateful praise.*

—JOHN 4:29;
— ——— 20:25;
— ——— 11;
— ——— 9

II
MANIFEST

— for Don Metz

TWO CHETS

Let us face it.
Life is stranger
than our inventions, being the ground
thereof, being the limit,

being the promise and instantaneous close.
We sip its baffling springs.
There I was,
just driving down

route 22 at the corner
where it dips below Calvin's house.
No matter that you don't know him;
this doesn't mean a thing.

I was simply following Chet
toward the river.
I knew him by the way he cocked
his head, and his silly swordfish hat.

As if he had ever seen the ocean!
I knew his truck,
and how he rode ever so slowly
(may God bless

such instances of decency!)
because he knew himself
driving drunk as usual.
On the decline,

he looked in his mirror
and made his customary little sign
—not quite a wave—with two fingers.
He sat small in the pickup's chassis,

which was small itself against Mt. Bower,
granite moraine,
bleak, dismal,
though I know it foot by foot, from its foot

across the narrow lane
by the Andersons' diner
up to where it's nothing
but slag and skinny pine.

(From there you can see back this way
to Mt. Held and the right-wing Governor's farm.
If there were nothing
else to do so, his example would warn—

Never say *simple* or *simply*.)
I felt the usual comfort
of being known by others, knowing them.
I didn't think to be scared of lyrical faith,

to be glad I didn't have it
nor, quite, its absence. Then
along came this Chevy S-10.
I could see its driver's empurpled face,

he drove so slowly up the other lane,
splashing the minuscule puddles.
I saw the absurd long bill of his cap,
like a round-point spade.

I saw its familiar angle,
and the head's as well.
Both of us kept on moving,
but here's the little part I want to tell:

It was Chet, Chet waved,
and when I looked back
to where I was going,
that other Chet ahead of me was gone

without a trace.
Not that Chet is anything much.
Not that I am either.
Yet ahead there was nothing

but the insignificant town
against the mountain,
whose freshets ran athwart each other
down the famished and ravaged face,

falling, falling out of the dark scrawny
evergreen bushes.
Don't remind me
how low this ranks among the wonders,

how trivial it is, how slight
the slender waters' singing rushes,
whatever I may have imagined.
Let me ask you, Stranger:

what are those flashes
when something happens and unhappens
all at once, and you see life,
its starts, its odd reverses?

AT THE FLYFISHER'S SHACK

A structure, yes. You'd hardly say a house.
I say he loved it, though, the man who died here.
(In truth he seemed to pay it small attention.)
I find a blue-dun hackle neck he used,
some orange fur he pilfered from a kitten,
a tying bobbin hanging from its thread there,
a vise that held his hooks, the verdigris
collecting now where silver plate once was.

   A cap. A pair of boots. Impressions, these,
of his career, or were they first suggestions
of its end?

          Outside, a great tree bends,
a pine that drew the children whose amusements
wrought the dips and swerves its branches show,
town kids whose absence I might call a function
of how the pine grows old with grace. Just so,
the old man's pain (and always there was plenty—
the son collapsed on a baseball field at twenty,
the grandson whom he raised who shot himself:
   always there is plenty. . . .). Pain also
might seem a part of what he chose from life,
a wage. He bent a little,

              then a little
more. I see in mind the nose that dropped
toward the fly he tied, and ever nearer
every season; clear as tears, a bauble
gathers at its tip. I know this ought
to be grotesque or droll, and is and isn't.
He couldn't wipe it off, in concentration
rapt, in study, building something fine—
   ephemeral, he knew, mere fur and feather.

Was this man good? Like us he was and wasn't.
He'd tie a half a dozen,
       then would choose
two or maybe three that struck him right.
The cabin kept on falling all around,
but I am here to say the man could tie
whenever he'd a mind! And then he died,
the way we do. At least there's one sure truth.
A basket that he wove of brown ash roots
still holds hooks he wrapped and then unchose.

  I meant to speak of nothing but the chosen.
And yet they speak as well, all the unchosen,
such distinction
      —keen in mind—now blurred
like any other. How he'd criticize
the work of his own hand or of another's!
"But it comes down, I guess, to presentation.
Boy," he'd often tell me, "there are days
a bungled pattern's just what they prefer."
A little breeze now lisps its way downriver,
intent or not to shake the old pine's limbs.

  Woven, it appears, of very air,
inside the old friend's closet there's a coat.
Was it too much in vogue
       or not enough?
His family's photos peer unclear through dust;
I wonder what impression they have here.
His bobbin swings along its vague ellipse.
The chosen and unchosen: flies or lives;

  obsessions; patterns; things put on or not;
paths of sure intent
     or otherwise.

CLOUDED EVENING, LATE SEPTEMBER

Confusion of song. On the radio,
"The autumn leaves drift by my window."
    "Ba-ba, black sheep, have you any wool?"—

Over his crib, the mobile's tune.
And tumbling into the tub I fill,
    Sh sh: persistent rush of water.

His mother's away. Does her milk rush down?
She's away. *Sh sh*— persistent, I proffer
    A hush. I imagine her pained expression,

The way she folds her slender arms
To cover the stain. The child's all vision,
    All eyes in his blurry focus upon

Drifting stars and beasts of wool
Above his bed in their quiet collisions.
    "The autumn leaves of red and gold . . .

"I see her face, the summer kisses,
The sunburned hands I used to hold."
    The fall is sudden, real, cold.

And suddenly too my eyes are filled
With whatever it is that seems bound to tumble.
    I lift the child, who splashes and babbles,

As foolish there in scented water
As yesterday his older sister,
    Begging to swim past dusk in a lake.

Rocky, frigid, dark as ocean.
Soon The Bear and The Bull and Orion
    Would gallop over, the sky all flaked

With their brilliance. I wondered if I might save her
Should a wave come rushing down, wind-driven.
    Mere child herself, she yet imagines

Me of all people to be a master.
Harvest of song in late September:
    One for the little girl; one for my dame

(How is it that *absence* can crowd the brain?);
One for the infant who pukes and mewls;
    And one somehow adrift in clouds,

Like softest wool all gathered round.
Like softest wool, indeed, but full
    Of something bound to tumble down.

QUESTIONS OF EMPATHY WAY UPSTATE

Can we guess that this ground is québecois?
Is that why its heavy rocks are gathered
dead center, and not in Yankee walls?
Do crops of these pasture rocks grow nightly?
Does anything happen here that matters?

Can we feel if the farmer feels despair?
That isn't—is it?—very likely.
Just now can we guess that he's looking through
his window toward that shrine out there?
That now he mutters, *Tout foutu?*

Is it really a bathtub, stood on end?
Can we guess that the farmer painted it
a hue that seemed appropriate—
angel blue, as the label said?
Does Baptiste moan, *She's dead, She's dead?*

Can it really be a grot for The Virgin
—plastic figure, suction-cup base?
What is the ground of this, our vision?
Can we see it under the locust trees?
And do those tatterdemalion leaves

anneal themselves to it in storm,
pale, like chalkings of grounded birds?
Why do we call this man Baptiste?
Do even plastic features grow worn?
Are they as heavy and worn as his,

now that his little Louise is gone?
For him, has too much happened here?
Lou-Lou, Lou-Lou, est-elle disparue?
Does heavy rain fall? Does he mumble a prayer
at our Bathtub Lady of Angel Blue

for everything to rise on air?

PIETÀ

It is not any single version
that moves me so, but all: great Buonarotti's
no more than the one I bought as if to mock it
    on its smarmy Venetian postcard whose cake-pink Virgin's

tears bring me tears. That He is grown
(as much an adult, you could say, as she)
is part of what weighs on me.
    But who's it *for,* this grief of mine,

this mourning? The fact of touch. And the mystery—
sublime or vulgar, sobbing or stoic,
the two are ever other. Crude, heroic,
    distracted, whatever: in every rendering I see,

so other. Of course there's sadness that a mother
should posture with her blasted seed, but fineness,
surely, too. I wonder if Kliney,
    my oddly named and fated brother,

before the hemorrhage fully blacked his brain,
felt some such mother-touch.
Once he'd left the breast, there wasn't much
    by way of laying-on of hands

between those two. This poem
assigns no blame to either party. I
am the one who writes it, I who've shied
    as much as he from home,

as much beyond her reach.
Or no, not quite as much. I'm still alive.
I don't know how I've reached this dim surmise
    that as the pale tube leached

its useless glucose nurture from a sack
and the EEG's thin scribble flattened out
she dropped the bright steel rail and put
    her fingers to his face—but that

is the thing that touches me beyond all reason.
That, and the counter-vision, that as in life,
in death as well the two were stiff
    and formal, blood between them

too much, and years, and that the Anglo-
Saxon sequesters passion out of sight.
Does everyone sometimes? That night,
    dazed farmers, as they angled

headstrong herds to fold, may well have mumbled
clichés on weather, games and levies,
like us when things, as the saying goes, get heavy.
    And heavy they'd been. Earliest miracle

in fact was maybe that Mary was enlightened
—in every sense the word can carry—
enough to hold him there, to parry
    the nuisance thrusts of insects, cleanse him, frighten

away the innocent rubbernecking kids.
Miracle of grace—or was it courage?
The funeral lacked all cant or flourish.
    You sat erect there, Mother. What you did

three days before in the darkened ward
I've never learned. This is a kind of guessing,
maybe a way of asking.
   To hold a ruined man who's yours

as husband, friend or lover
can never be. . . .
It is the unthinkable *notion* that touches me,
   as much your flesh as the ruined Brother.

The notion and the posture, and he within it,
manchild, or maybe not at all.
As I might be. Pity. *Pietà.*
   Mercy. I could think to want it.

FOR THE SOLITARY

So that's why they've said he's thinner. Cancer.
Now it sounds like a pun, and meaner,
What someone remarked years back about him:
"He isn't much. You'll barely see him."
That's all I was told, latecomer, stranger,

But that he'd always yearned for Alaska,
Had coveted its mystic scale,
Who lived on trifling Sutter's Knoll
Beside his stone-and-vegetable patch,
Who paints today his shoebox shack,

Out of hiding at last, in bright fall air.
I spy. I wonder what brings him here.
I wonder if he's concluded his hamlet
Contains far more than he ever imagined—
Acorn, antler, ridgeline, rock,

Great-fledged turkeys with swollen crops,
Grays, profuse in this late November
And variegated as blues in midsummer,
Black marble of night, dawn's poppy sun.
I might go on. He might go on

To apply exorbitant ornamentation
As planets school toward winter positions,
And spring's grown broods leave tracks in gravel,
And ducks on the sloughs churn upward, startled
By their own splendor of plumage, it seems,

And frost-emancipated seeds
Troop to ground or stream in cascade.
As things prepare to go spare they explode
Or shine: the fatted cattle's ordures,
The lapidary mounds of fodder,

Jet flies drifted by southern windows,
Worms in the dark of their ruinous tunnels.
At daybreak the brilliant roosters cry:
Any day now! Any day!
And yet, I see, for all of that,

He chooses a dim, transparent shellac.
O, if only he would have it,
His circumstance might be Alaska—
Vast, obscure, particular.
Is the dark of the pine groves any darker?

Oak-bark is nuanced with jadelike green.
Something perhaps in me alone—
A stranger now as much as ever—
Desires a luminous closing figure.
You'll barely see him will be *you didn't.*

He isn't much will be *he wasn't.*

LATE SEASON

This was the last I'd trouble the ducks this season:
there'd be skim-ice on the slues
and later, snow come down from Canada, horizontal.
There might be some luck, a little . . .
no, more. It was already there, beforehand:
dirt road near dawn, canoe
snubbed in the pickup's bed,

and in my lap the great good head
of my dog, the blood in his graying muzzle
a pulse in my leg as we bucked the ruts.
And, come down from a Canada even farther,
music, local notices, news of the weather—
the radio's early report. I imagined the struggle
of a farmer there. Up like me. *Good mutt,*
I whispered. I scratched

the retriever's neck.
It was warm. Reception good. The farmer leaned
in mind into winds that they say
can straighten a tow-chain out behind a tractor.
I liked driving tractor-slow, imagining that weather.
Plenty of time. Down here, whatever the wind,
I could count for now on a milder day.
I was forty-five. I liked how the a.m. signal

said something about what it was to be fuddled,
or rather how static fell away when your object was
    clear:
getting from house to barn and back in a gale;
getting the decoys out before you froze;
getting into the proper kinds of clothes
to meet a day. Getting it right. A cold time of year,
but for now I was snug behind the wheel,
and already I could envision

the redleg Blackduck blown down and past in migration,
the reach of a wave from the farther shore of the river
toward me, where I'd sit, alone but for the dog.
Wave like a single important announcement.
A blind of fragile reeds, and all around it
the signs of how we must seek to save forever
what we receive of what goes by: a buck
who has left his ghostly track in slush and mud;

gleam of low sun in old blood;
spent shells, drifting clumps of insubstantial feather,
gone in a moment, abiding in the mind;
feel of a dog companion's eager breathing
turned to frost on your cheek, then melting to nothing.
Later the awful snow would come to the river,
and later the careful blind no longer stand,

nor dog, nor duck, nor I, nor Canada farmer.

ROADSIDE, FEBRUARY

Sleet against that rabbit-hound's house since dawn
—if we could hear—
must sound like a mean little gun:
rat-tat-tat-tat.
A single line of tracks, out and back,
to and from the frozen yellow smear
and the skimped hard stools that mark the end of the tether.
Are you from here?

Not of course that a dog can answer,
but if it's a bitch,
you must know he calls her "Queenie" or "Lady";
"King" for a male, or something like "Tuffy" maybe.
Do you know the owner?
The empty letterbox says "Fitch."
It's an age since we heard from the songbirds, saw the flowers.
Do you miss them?

I regret when they were here
—almost it seems before the birth of Desire—
I scarcely paid attention.
Before the dark,
before he has finished his broken
six of beer,
wan, singular, Fitch
will make his way out over the slick.

He'll bear a dish of small coarse pellets like pills.
Then back to his shack where they have married,
soot and ice, in his dormer's valleys.
Only a tiny *crunch crunch*
might possibly tell
between the poor dog's normal
shiver and moan
and the sound of its eating, if anyone were to hear.

(My talk is silent of course—to myself alone.)
Imagine how thin the animal
must be inside!
In the TV's glare
in Fitch's cabin, even the color of light
is cold—snow-blue.
The shingles swell with quiet disaster.
The sleet makes a dam on the roof.

Everywhere water comes through.
Nearby, a sodden chickadee puffs,
as if trying to swell himself grander.
Are you from here?
If so, just think how tough
we thought we had it in December,
in the dark of the year.
Remember the TV lady?

She'd click her teeth and point at the map,
declaring, "Winter's scarcely begun,
and already cheeks are rosy."
Her daily command,
all cheerful: "Bundle up."
Well, we were wrong,
those mornings when we leaned against the wind,
making our way from house to car.

We bitched at the roads to our jobs, slick,
the traffic barely moving.
Look at the roof, the beagle.
Desire or despair:
we didn't know nothing.
Look at Fitch's tin weathervane eagle
tethered, transfixed
by an icy axle,

and the gaping mailbox, canted into the ditch.

MANIFEST

—litany: winter walk

In evergreens, wind-riven,
    whose blaze-orange wounds
    at limb and crown certify passion;
In the mitten-wool taste
    of snow you scoop to your mouth
    because—so you imagine—you thirst;
In illogical woodpeckers' laughter,
    in their swooping flight,
    that suggests assertion crossed by doubt;
In rough-frozen rims of tracks
    the animals left in the dark preceding
    nights, whose meaning needs no glozing;
In the hue of a beech
    —neither quite somber gray
    nor placid blue—that teases all sight and belief;
In the way this sun at solstice
    jumps up from the hill
    and asks no reading, but affirmation in the chill;
In the ermine who fought the owl,
    resisting negation:
    alone now, scarlet in snow—conspicuous, stiffened;
In the steam of your coffee at dawn,
    pale testimony to addiction, harmless,
    perhaps more so than others you want;
In one long-damaged knee
    whose cartilage resists your walk, and warns
    against a mock-tranquility;
In the bland and sweet obedience
    of your dogs, which raises questions
    that touch on your worthiness, competence;

In the warmth (to which you'll return)
     of shelter, so easily canceled should your fuel
     withhold its fire—a residue of the sun;
In fire, that has the power and glory
     of "the things that have been made," as St. Paul saith,
     commanding faith, however airy;
In warmth and shelter and fire,
     to which of course you will return,
     for which you are whetting desire;
In desire, whose quenching is life
     and death, as poets used to say—
     by enjoinder and designation: *husband, wife;*
In this cheery fall of siskins
     to an earth that you'd thought barren: in their number,
     that may be somewhere counted, their busy-ness;
In their vanishing
     —before you can count them yourself—
     that sermonizes vanity;
In the far waw of a power saw
     that binds on a softwood's sap, congealed:
     the logger swears profanely, we are not healed;
In the warming recollection of your children,
     for whose sake you pray as you can for death
     to have no dominion, that you are forgiven.

III
MUSEUM

—for Catherine

PIANISSIMO

Although I've claimed to know the language well,
So gentle is his call, so low—a vowel,
A breath—small wonder that its pain escapes me.

I've left behind my glasses: when he falls,
Beside a vineyard, in a field, downhill,
At first I lose him. Tiny in the poppies,

He seems a figure from some magic tale,
Flower stems the bars of his soft jail.
Can that sweet call have meant, *Signore, save me?*

Just now I might be anywhere at all,
A tourist only, from another world.
I might be hiking any other valley.

What he whispers next I can't quite tell,
Though once I claimed I knew this language well.
I think, though, every other word's *morire.*

Things seem far too still, as in some spell
Or dream in which one needs to run and fails.
I'm locked in gentle dusk in the Chianti,

The broom in bloom, whose magical sweet smell
Configures with some Angelus's bell.
At that, where might I run? I lift him gently,

Like a baby. On a ruined wall,
A lizard shows a pulse, redundant, small,
Like tickings of the watch I've left behind me,

On my holiday, with time to kill.
Only such slight fibrillations tell
He lives at all. O spell, O sweet *far niente:*

Lost to deed and word alike, I fall
Into your snares. This stillness overall
Will find his heart at last. My will betrays me.

An ox uphill lows gently from a stall.
The tiny man breathes softly still, *Signore,*
No longer, though, I think, to me at all.

Or is the word, I wonder, still *morire?*
I'm just a tourist here in the Chianti,
So much of this soft dialect escapes me.

ON MUNSON ISLAND

—in mem. MKL, again

Barefoot in haunt-white dust
We've thickened or thinned
But the same
Sun behind us

Decades gone
Far from shore   There seems no change
We play horsehoes   *All but one*
Stakes farther apart

Than back then
They'll be close together again
Don't mind   Don't lose heart
The game's not the point

It could be tennis   chess
Or no game
There won't
Be a doubling on *stakes*

On *horseshoes*
Only same old horseshoes
Nothing I think to say
Of *luck*   Their steel is steel

Not *endurance*   Nothing stands
For anything here   No appeal
To some loved yellow picture
There could be   but never mind

(One has us here as one
Little-brothers-and-sisters
—Now again *all but one*
The same—

Each holds a small perch The sun
Shines behind
Each fish each girl
Each boy translucent

All rib and bone all but transparent
That light appeals
Never mind None of that matters)
Ellen throws a leaner

See Ellen smile
Jane laughs but I think she's piqued
A competitor's manner
Jake quiet ever hard to read

Remember the gone one
My tosses seem random
I'm poor at games
That's not the point

Not the point
That like then
Through whole seasons
I've thrown throw will throw no ringers

Nor that unfathomable Jake
Jane Ellen have and will
If I threw one what a wonder
If from the waves of the same old lake

Some dear ghost rose
A wonder as well
Never mind   Wonder is here   close
The same   *all but one*   us

Same sun   now   same dust

MUSEUM

recalling George MacArthur
and Donald Chambers

Small thunder cuts my autumn doze on the porch.
Trotting by, two thoroughbreds—skittish, slender.
Dream is at once a heavy and delicate thing.

Donald's wrinkles could hold a week of rain.
Every fall, he told me, he'd bleed his horse.
A horse's waters thicken, summering over.

Or did he say he bled her after winter?
He spoke so much, so often, I ought to remember.
He said and said and said, I wasn't there.

A horse don't mind, she didn't mind, he said.
He'd make a jutting movement into air.
You put the knife-point, quick as you could, inside.

A Belgian would barely flinch, God was his witness.
He swore the roan mare didn't care.
Only a little prick in the palate's softness.

It's America, it's 1988.
Shy, the thoroughbred pair, and thin in the leg.
Soft and bright, the rider's clothes—like mine.

Queenie, he whispered, she lowered her trunk of a neck.
Her look was almost bored, she seemed to yawn.
There stood a barrel, and blood came pouring down.

You needed to stanch it with alum right on time.
A horse was a thing you wanted not to lose.
By God you wanted a rugged horse back then.

Back then the trees got bigger than they do.
My road was just a path in the swamp, of course.
I wasn't there, repeat, not there, repeat.

You can't remember somebody now by a horse.
Not by a horse that really works, at least.
All I recall is Donald telling me of it.

Queenie, he'd whisper, repeating her name, he loved it.
You can't recall a person by a canoe.
I'm thinking now of George as well, awake.

Not a canoe you use, you really use.
You had to portage then from here to the lake.
Riverman, river of words, song-singer, Bard.

The only roads were tote roads then, George said.
Repeating himself, repeating, I wasn't there.
You could borrow the loan of a horse if you were tired.

A timber horse, well-bled and -fed, was strong.
A Belgian would hardly pay a canoe attention.
You lashed it onto a sledge and drove it on.

George and Donald were there, who now are gone.
And this may be the realm of imagination.
When the Blackducks flew from the lake they covered the sun.

When a he-bear coughed in the woods, the great flanks trembled.
You threw wet trout on the garden to feed your corn.
You bled a horse in autumn, or was it spring?

Good smell of flesh and blood, haydust in the hovel.
Even in January the flanks would steam.
Vaporous stuff of New England. Imagination.

Useless, swift and helpless, the thoroughbreds.
Dream's domain; talk unto song; museum.
You have to make sure that too much blood don't spill.

They told me so, they laughed, they frowned, they said.
There were rocks, rapids, currents you couldn't feel.
Solid things and spectral, redundant winds.

There were widow-makers, limbs that fell without sound.
Sometimes, though, the horses seemed to hear.
Sometimes they'd bolt, and a ton of horse can maim.

That much horse is a delicate thing all the same.
So Donald always suggested, I wasn't there.
You could fix any boat you didn't completely lose.

Sometimes I lose it, even the shadow from slumber.
Canvas and cedar, ash ribs, gunwales of spruce.
Mist, recalls—Donald and George, New England.

Horses, canoes, talk, men, museum.
Thunder: wood-scrap, green cloth going under.
The old men's regal faces could hold the rain.

One twitches the horse's lip, the knife jabs in.
Riders wave to me from the road all cheerful.
I think the Belgian mare's big legs will buckle.

I think we're late, and blood brims over the barrel.
Its stain is the shade of these Indian summer maples.
It's 1988, the canoe is fragile.

The spindly trot comes liquid through autumn air.
Words I repeat and repeat for George and Donald.
I say and say and say who wasn't there.

D-DAY ODE FOR DEAN

At first, up on the scaffold,
he needed a pull of his gin.
Was this the world he'd fought for?
He opened the paint-can, baffled.
Not even paint, but stain,

A tint like earth's by his trench.
Why so grim, these owners?
He sighed: he was just an old soldier.
He yawned, his pale eyes clenched:
tears, streaks, blurs.

The blackflies, not yet started;
his bosses, not moved in.
Peace, and its icon bird,
fluting: That was more like it.
To coast a bit above land.

Morning. Pinks. Yellows.
Everything airborne. Odd,
it had dawned like this at St. Malo:
farm animals over salt sod,
like the ship riding harbor-fog's billows

that he hoped might float him homeward.
Guarding its earthen den,
now a far fox yammered.
He'd been a boy in these hills,
when the house was Grandfather's barn.

He knew it couldn't go on—
the gin all day, the pills.
The stain on this morning's brush
resembled dried blood or sludge.
There! that bird-note again.

Slurred, sweet, airy.
Despite the reek from the can,
he could smell the perished dairy.
Survival was secondary
to rest; he'd lain down at will,

prepared in the night to be killed,
but had wakened to wondrous calm:
colors, sheep, cattle.
Where was the fierceness of battle,
all its wreck and hurry and violence,

ruins, shrapnel, bombs?
If another might fear the near-silence,
or at least be made uneasy,
here he was, a survivor,
feeling merely dizzy.

Today, he knew he could hover.
That fusillade—only a woodpecker.
Ghostly mild beasts from the farm
were treading middle air.
He meant to join them there

and never fall to harm.

WINTER TOURNAMENT

Our daughters' lay-ups shivered rim or air;
White, their sighs at free throws; passes were
Tropes for awkward prayer.
                                    Georgianna watched
From comfortless cold bleachers set on blocks.
We didn't cry despair or yelp with pain.
Now Coach exhorts the girls to dream of gain
From rout; he clears his throat; the loss, he says,
Should "light a fire" somewhere inside the players.
His figure's wrong. Georgianna once was young.
Like them. And he was too. And we. All wrong. . . .

Who'll go on dreaming jump shots, bullet-sure?
Georgianna? No such certainty for her,
In dreams or anywhere,
                                    I dare imagine.
(To tell the truth, we haven't even spoken.)
Yet here she was, like all of us, to cheer
Or grieve. It's clumsy. Monuments to care,
These mothers, mostly: gone to flesh or bone,
But lovely too. Back-bent, the skinny ones
Have hugged themselves beside their warmer neighbors,
Who've tried to hide sagged parts in upright postures.

Georgianna's simply worn—not thin, not fat.
Someone should prop *her* up or hold her tight.
Or so she feels tonight,

                                        I speculate,
As we collect our children. Those defeats—
Goals rejected, miscues, slips and fouls—
May work their disenchantment on our girls.
Yet I daresay that we imagine beauties
Are at their truest when they're so ungainly.
We cling to daughters, and to that surmise,
As carefully we tiptoe over ice

—Clownish in the dark—to heating cars.
At least in awkwardness they are most ours.

AMPUTEE

—Good Friday, Caledonia County

The yard crew screamed for the other truck.
Joe brought it and picked the load off Jack with the crane.
A wonder, how quickly he did.
But he could have waited years, for all it did:
powder and marrow already, the bone;
and the flesh—mat, thread, muck.

Now Jack's wife must work a job.
His mother's helping at home, who's come to think
that somehow she was there
to watch the long-logs shift, and she was there
to see them tumble over bunk-stakes.
She claims the binders didn't grab.

Then Joe got down by Jack on his knees.
Joe Maloney . . . Joe One-and-Only.
The others turned from the wounds.
Common stuff enough for loggers, wounds,
like sawdust, pine knots, skinny money.
But they couldn't make themselves look at this.

Jack calls her *monkey* and *mountain goat*—
his daughter, his baby—or *angel*. She loves to climb.
"Like you did," moans his mother.
It's been a year to the day. Jack loves his mother,
but she's worn him down these months with gloom.
And wasn't it *he* who'd caught that load?

He'd stood there blessing the song of engines.
He'd be home soon; the trucks were stacked and going.
Coals still throbbed in the yard.
The crew had kept a fire, for the landing yard
was chilly: heartbreak spring winds blowing.
The glow of the embers caught Jack's attention.

The soft ditch sucked at the big rig's tire.
Jack's mother slumps, seeing it all, she imagines.
His daughter giggles, climbs.
Joe was the one to come down, who used to climb,
back when he logged the west-slope Tetons.
"It's a different pretty out there," he declared,

"but pretty." Now Joe drove a truck.
Jack's daughter mounts the dresser, couch and counter,
anything that stands.
For now, her father only sits or stands.
Bless Joe for kneeling down, no matter,
thinks Jack, who'll find some other work.

His mother says the hemlock fell
as though it *aimed* at her son's right thighbone.
The God who's plagued her mind
and life had simply taken it in mind,
and there you were, hell and damnation!
Jack lets her chatter: what the hell?

His daughter's aiming ever higher.
He'd seen Joe feel his shirt sometimes for nitro.
Joe by God was all right.
So he'd tell you: "By God I'm all right."
The coals had cooled to indigo.
The dusk had been going dark, and darker. . . .

Beautiful, though. Beautiful now.
The light-poles' crosses. The knolls. The sky.
The trees beyond Jack's window.
The hard young stars, aglow. And through the window,
he'll watch his weary wife arrive,
who glows as well. She sees him through,

his daughter too, who's bound to climb,
who dreams of rising to rafter and collar beam.
A ghost pain makes Jack jump.
His crutch falls away with a clack. His daughter jumps
to help him. Angel. Joe came down.
Jack's mother sighs. His family's home.

SUN, RISING

You're wearing me.   The phrase still mumbles itself, stilted, half-stern.
I forget what I'd done, but Father, I'd grown too big for you to handle.
Down on a knee,   winded, you sized me up. A world was dismantled,

not to cohere   again. Not for a time. The short years blew
away, you   were gone, and I was hurricaned into today.
Winded up here   myself, high, in the snow, although it's May.

Nothing but wind.   That, and the little freshets fossicking seaward,
and fog falling earthward.   That, and the old, tuneless voice of Despair.
I've climbed again,   as if to clamber into a lighter air.

For all its weight,   memory keeps pace, however; it even leads.
I remember the floods of spring, and how, in our canvas slip of canoe,
we'd ride the spate   until it flattened into the lake's May blue;

I was ahead   back then, whatever that may signify.
In fact the sky   and water so mirrored each other it made me dizzy,
light in the head: up, down, before, behind—all hazy,

and hazier still   the prospect since. I wear the smeary lenses
a life imposes: house, wife, job, money, babies.
Even this hill,   to me so *known,* dissolves itself into mazes.

I'm astray.   I rebuke myself for wandering up in the dark.
Moss on the bark   of trees up here grows heedless in all directions.
I could pray, but the murmur within and silence outside are distraction,

and that I make   myself the stuff I'm fleeing. I love my children
and the noble woman   at whom too often, stilted, I carp and whine
as a dog will rake   the very plaster affixed to anneal rent skin

58

(though I figure the gesture more often as a bird's who plucks its breast
to warm the nest).   No wonder the fog. No wonder the vanished path.
No wonder the hindward   scrutiny, the talon-grip of the past.

Shouldn't there be   a term for mourning? Shouldn't the trip I ruined
in the sullen cabin,   the rain I cursed, as if you were to blame—
shouldn't I see   them all, as they seemed to fall, again

fly up, away?   Shouldn't the claw withdraw? Shouldn't the tent
in which we spent   those campfired evenings that should have worked,
somehow today   take wing? Up here I see it, odd green ark,

befeathered, rising   into the cloaking clouds over Moody Mountain.
And now that the vision   has started its antic, improbable course,
I'm surmising   plumes as well on the dreary, sleet-stung hearse,

on fender and fin   of the ludicrous 1950s automobile
in which we wheeled each morning to school, silent, encumbered, slow,
and back again   at evening, nothing to say, and nothing now;

and even the small   cedar-and-fabric canoe: its gunwales burst open,
and there grow pinions!   and off we fly more lightly than on the lake,
never to fall.   And I will imagine, if only for vision's sake,

wings on you   (as in a Sunday Schooler's phantasmic design),
and trailing behind   —or are they ahead? are they below or above?—
the little woes   and the great, angelified, transformed by Love,

till the very air   is wings, is quiet no more, is wings and song.
And now the sun   is flying up and through the pass, suffusing
the outlook near   and far. And if the way for me is still confusing,

I'll find it now.   As God will witness me, there is a feather,
sky-blue, Father,   propped in a pure-white drift. I drop to a knee.
I'm wearing you,   this feather in my hat, and whatever else may be.

OVER BROGNO

If from behind the stars
the perilous archangel came down,
our thunderous heartbeats would kill us.
—RILKE

After the ten or twenty
    quiet minutes
        within the empty
church at San Giovanni,
           the lisping wavelets of the Como arm
           of the lake even less audible
           than the little implosions of dove-flight
           in the tower above like the shuffle
           of cards in a deck—

After my bourgeois
    reverie and rote prayers
        for the absent ones,
wife, children, friends,
           the lungs and torso at length light
           as wings as thought was transformed
           by consciousness of the cosmos below,
           the thronged dead, their buoyant
           deep dust

beneath soft stone
    on which I sat
        all weightless now in the pew—
the bells of noon
        had the *ploosh* sound of iron anchors
        cast over into water.
        I stepped out onto the dazzled piazza,
        near blind to the chic *ragazza*
        who smiled a greeting

as she passed
    to the wharf's corner
        where she'd eat and read her glossy review.
Her womanhood weighted me too,
        and thus I made my sudden decision
        to turn, rise, go
        south to the snowy mountain
        along the ancient mule paths,
        avoiding the heavy

trucks, clutched
    lovers, cars
        so close I could almost touch them
on the wire-thin limestone
        roads banked high with rock, where escape
        seemed all but hopeless.
        I wanted to rise above all, withdraw
        from millennia's mulched refuse
        underneath me,

innocent as it was,
      innocent as the Virgin
            whose icons at every
bridge across the *torrente*
                were littered with candle, flower, coin—
                earthy leavings and spillings
                of quick and dead alike, moving
                back and forth and back
                along these tracks

like the bent
      illiterate *contadino*
            of whom I asked directions,
who courtly and gravely gestured:
                "At every fork, choose a way that climbs,
                if you must." To him there clung
                sweet dung, dirt, dust,
                as to others I passed, whom passing,
                I commended to God,

Addio. At which
      they would bow in respect,
            it seemed, but seemed bemused,
as if the expression I used
                signalled not greeting but intention.
                Did I think I was climbing *à Dio?*
                Did they smile because it was odd to encounter
                someone like me over Brogno?
                Or at the superstition

that the higher powers
   are something one has
     to seek in a higher order?
But they returned to their labors.
     Enough had passed on these mountain paths
     that another oddness could pass.
     Somewhere within my heart I thanked them,
     for only a troubled abstraction
     could have been my answer

if they had asked me
   where I was going.
     And what was this humming, far past the final
boulder-built hovel?
     There on the summit, in the absence of wind,
     the tall tower, the unfleshed
     skull and bones on the chilling sign
     —*Pericolo di morte!*
     And something seen

or seeming seen,
   an immanence, an aura.
     I thought beyond
to our time's angelic throngs:
     What deadly secrets? What secret soarings?
     What particles abroad?
     What specters of light that is more than light?
     Brogno far below,
     its inn and bar,

and I up there,
      and what radio waves winging by
          and bearing what lethal
abstraction from what capital,
         what lecture hall, what briefing room?
         Clamorous heartbeat, its clap
         within like thunder. Without, the Angel.
         I felt the heart must burst
         or draw me down

to cottage and shack,
         to human traffic,
         where souls move close to ground.

ANOTHER AUTUMN, AND

Again the trees' loud story
                quietens, grounded;
at roadside, tumbled foliage
                scatters, whispers,
again the world is sinking
                into night,
and further minor
                pastoral nullity:
the shadows lengthen fast,
                and so on. Ended,
composition will seem
                to have been erasure,
the whole a notebook's
                leaf left white.

I take our little boy
                along with me,
a two-year-old, too young
                I think to care
about originality.
                He kicks
a weary crackle
                from red maples here,
pale poplars there. The way
                the mind falls back,
falls *up,* seems both at once
                eccentric and banal.
He kicks. You kicked. I kicked.
                We kick the leaves.

And once these things we did
                 seemed fine and final,
seemed a turning over
                 of something new.
Father, it's '58.
                 It's been a struggle,
so you say, but now
                 it's on the rise.
I'm thinking other things,
                 but think this too.
You mean you've saved
                 your little company.
You're praising effort, family,
                 faith, and Ike.

My mind is racing:
                 I intend to write!
And you're my age, and don't
                 intend to die.
I turn to leave. I love you;
                 it is just. . . .
My blond boy wants and doesn't
                 want to be
like me. I want to go
                 back to our house.
He doesn't, races on,
                 but turns to see
if I will follow.
                 I would recompose

the past and future. Now
               I whisper, "Home."
He kicks and shouts. He turns
               and races on.
And now I think he's growing
               like a weed.
I'd like to go and empty
               all the graves. . . .
And here the sun is low,
               and somewhere high,
and all that falls will vanish
               and abide.
And in the shadows
               he is shouting "Leaves!"

FOR FAITH

All had a look and meaning, she remembers.
The spirals of birds—adieu—in autumn's bluster.
Sun turning shadows from gray to black, and darker.
Notes on the brittle hymnal pages, signatures . . .
Clouds, swelled in the tawny highland pastures
till they looked like snow on sand.
Gales that boded fair or ugly weather,
and the northward lake's consequent moods and colors.
Or something indoors, like wood mites fretting the rafters.

The ancient organ's keys are chilly, tan,
but they warm and even brighten under her hand.
Crackle of August grasshoppers all through the land
so loud she feared that the timothy-stubble burned.
For prelude, something noble, *forte,* grand.
The tiny choir in her mirror,
sleep in their eyes. Can she stir them still? She can.
Outside, resplendent, scarlet in Sabbath sun,
a convertible-top Corvette: it's hers, who ran

with her lucent, blood-bay mare beside her father,
riding astride in the piquant vacations of Easter:
shine of mane in the breezes; gull-squawks; lather;
turf, puddle, saddlesoap, evergreen, leather;
new grass rolling in waves to mimic the water's.
Or the naked Cardinal Plant,
Oriental in hailstone-pearled northeasters.
Or a chirr in the pantry: the laboring separator.
And her voice, so achingly clear, that makes these over. . . .

Season after season, arriving, turned:
Summer's giant evenings, late to begin
and coming like fog or scent so stealthily on,
as playful, she hid with her restive dogs in the barn.
At *c* above staff, there's one odd pipe that groans.
She has been the familiar
of this organ a long long time: the stop that pretends
it is *vox humana,* the autonomous *f* that sounds
if you hold the leftmost pedal too far down,

or mutes itself in the tonic chord for *d*-minor.
So much of this depends upon the weather.
The muteness, as well, and the pallor of her father,
sprawled in mud next to a calf he'd delivered.
Staring at whitecaps through kitchen windows, Mother
wheezed in rhythm, her hands dropped listless beside her.
How throaty, the sports car's motor:
it's not, however, something she'll consider,
leaving it all behind.   She raises a finger,

hoping Janette of the quavery alto will note her,
will alter a flatness; or maybe she as director
will take her part and sing it louder and drown her.
And still Janette will love her. That's the wonder.
So I think—quiet as a mime in my corner—
dreaming I understand.
Now, as the anthem follows, she starts all over.
If I'm wrong, still something rich and grand must move her
and make that light a fool could see above her.

ABOUT THE AUTHOR

SYDNEY LEA is founder and senior editor of *New England Review* and *Bread Loaf Quarterly*. He has held fellowships from the Guggenheim and Rockefeller Foundations and has published three collections of poetry, most recently *No Sign,* and a novel, *A Place in Mind.* In addition, he has edited an anthology of critical essays on the poetry of Anthony Hecht, and has taught at Dartmouth, Yale, and the Bread Loaf Writers' Conference. He lives in New Hampshire with his wife, Robin Barone, who is a lawyer, and four children.